You hurt, I hurt

Understanding Bullying
through the eyes
of the bullied
and bullier

© Copyright September 2015, Families, Adult & Youth Life Awareness, LLC (FAYLA)
248 Columbia Turnpike, Suite 210, Florham Park, New Jersey 07932
All rights reserved. No part of this publication may be copied, reproduced,
stored in a retrieval system, or transmitted in any form or by any means ~~
electronic, mechanical, photocopy, or any other ~~ without the prior written permission
of Families, Adult & Youth Life Awareness, LLC (FAYLA)

You hurt, I hurt

Understanding Bullying
through the eyes
of the bullied
and bullier

by
Dana Kaspereen, Ph.D.
Jennifer Tursi, M.A.

illustrated by
Stacy Bober

Dear Counselor, Teacher, or Caretaker:
Bullying is a tough topic! It is even harder when you are involved! This book is designed to help stop bullying! Bullying can be stopped by becoming aware of what it really means and feels like through the eyes of BOTH the bullied and bullier. This book can be used one on one or in a small group setting.

How to use this book:

- With guidance by a counselor, teacher, or caretaker… start with THROUGH THE EYES OF THE BULLIED side.
- Use the book as a workbook and encourage the reader to write their feedback and comments right in the book.
- Discuss each page and topic regarding bullying.
- Make sure the reader understands the lesson before moving on.
- When this section is complete, flip the book around and start THROUGH THE EYES OF THE BULLIER side.
- Same steps apply.
- MOST IMPORTANTLY…BE PATIENT.

This book was created to be helpful, but it can also be very emotional and difficult at times. For readers who have been bullied or are bullying others, this is a time to reflect and observe their behaviors. Remember to be patient, understanding, and empathetic. We encourage each reader to learn what it is like to be either the bullied or the bullier, through their eyes…

 **Hi!**

My name is Conner!
I need a friend...

Are you a good listener?
I have been bullied at school.

Do you know what
bullying means?

What is bullying?

 I did not know what bullying meant either until it happened to me.

So let me tell you what I learned...

Bullying is when someone or a group of people purposely hurt another person through talk or touch.

The person being bullied might feel alone, scared and have trouble standing up for themselves.

This can happen over and over again unless someone tells an adult!

Guess what???

Anyone can be bullied.

It does not matter if you are a girl or a boy,

tall or short,

big or small.

How do you know if you are being bullied?

Great question!

Bullying can be through

TOUCH or **TALK**

pushing	name calling
punching	spreading rumors
shoving	teasing
kicking	yelling
tripping	laughing at someone to hurt their feelings
slapping	

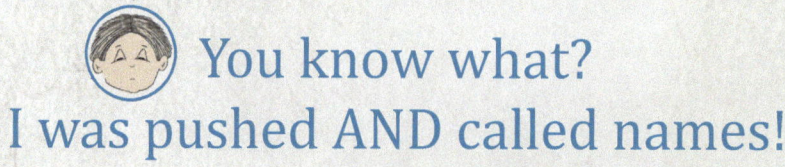 You know what?
I was pushed AND called names!

Bullying can
take place anywhere...

I mean ANYWHERE!

Can you guess some places
where bullying might happen?

Some places bullying can happen are...

- **in your classroom**
- **on the playground**
- **in the hallways**

   or even...

- **on the bus**

 I was bullied in the cafeteria during lunch.

Why might someone pick on me?

Why am I being bullied?

Maybe the bully is...

- **jealous of me**
- **different than me**
- **trying to peer pressure me**
- **feeling bad about themself**
- **following others**
    Or maybe...
- **they have been or
  are being bullied too**

Whatever the reason...
it hurts!

PEER PRESSURE

JEALOUSY

SAD

ANGRY

Listen up!
If you have been bullied...

You are not alone!

You DID NOT cause the bullying to happen to you!

A lot of people get bullied at some point in their life.

 I felt like I was alone.

I did not realize my friend was being bullied too!

What can you do if you are being bullied?

- **tell a parent(s) or guardian**
- **tell your teacher**
- **tell a counselor**

    or

- **tell another adult you feel safe with.**

You can work together to make the bullying stop.

Be brave and talk about it.

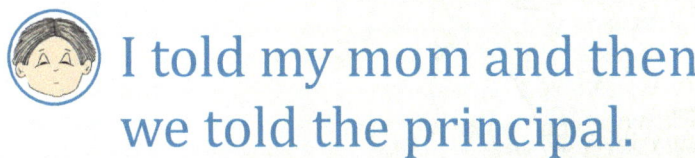 I told my mom and then we told the principal.

SAFETY STARS!

reach for the stars

It is important to know who you can trust and talk to if you are being bullied. You should have a safe person at every place you spend time.

Let's think...

write in the people you can trust at...
(use the blank stars for any place or person you can think of)

SAFETY CIRCLES!

to stop bullying tell a...

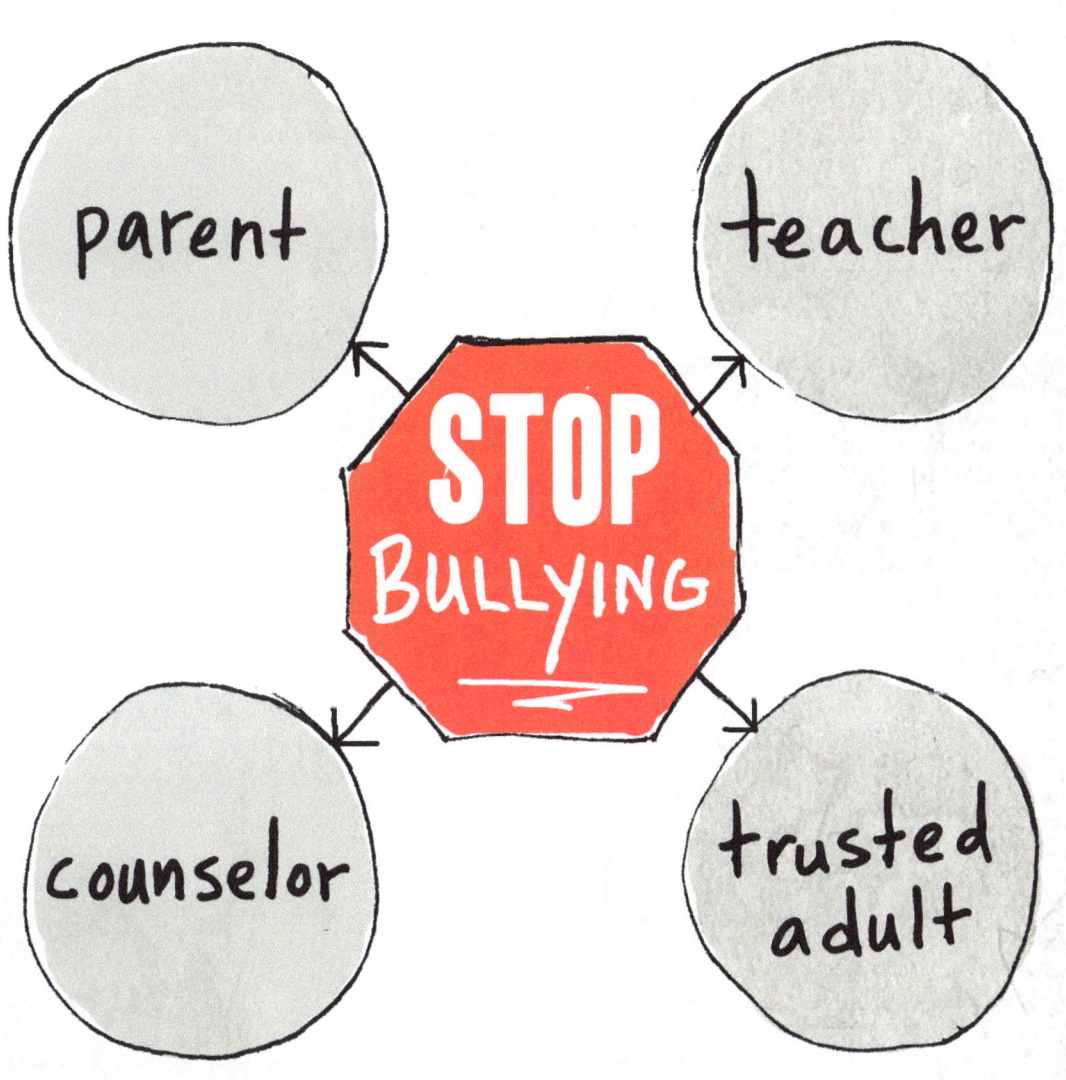

What can you do to feel better?

 **What I like to do is:**

- read a book
- play with my favorite toy
- talk to someone I love

Now it is your turn...

Tell me what you can do to feel better...

1. _____
2. _____
3. _____
4. _____
5. _____

Circle the face(s) that you would feel if you were bullied...

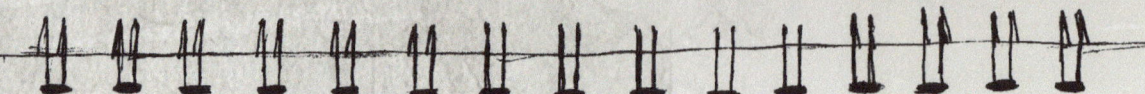

Draw a picture of how someone who is being bullied might feel.

What should you do if you are bullying someone?

First... STOP being a bully and either tell:

- **a parent(s) or guardian**
- **a teacher**
- **a counselor**
    or
- **another adult you trust**

You can work together to make the bullying stop and learn how to apologize.

You will feel much better!

Draw a picture of how someone who is the bully might feel.

Have you ever seen someone being bullied?

If so, here is what you do...

SEE:
ask yourself... is this **TALK** or **TOUCH** bullying?

SPEAK:
think back to your "SAFETY CIRCLES" and choose at least one person to tell about the bullying.

SAVE:
know you did the right thing and helped someone else. You are a HERO!

Why might my friends
be in trouble?

Are they also being a bully for just
standing there?

YES!

**It might be hard or you might be
scared... but, if you watch someone
being bullied, you need to
tell an adult!**

Laughing at a friend or telling them to
pick on someone is just as bad!
If you do not tell an adult about the
bullying you see, then you are part
of the bullying.

 My friends were not surprised
I got in trouble!

They said I was mean.

They were mad at me when they
got in trouble for not telling anyone.

They even got in trouble
for laughing.

If you have bullied someone before, it does not mean you are a bad person. Talk to a trusted adult about your feelings and why you are hurting another person.

Be brave and talk about it.

I got in trouble with the principal for bullying Conner! My dad had to come to school. I was in trouble at school AND at home. I was really sorry that I made Conner feel so bad.

SAFETY CIRCLES!

to stop bullying tell a...

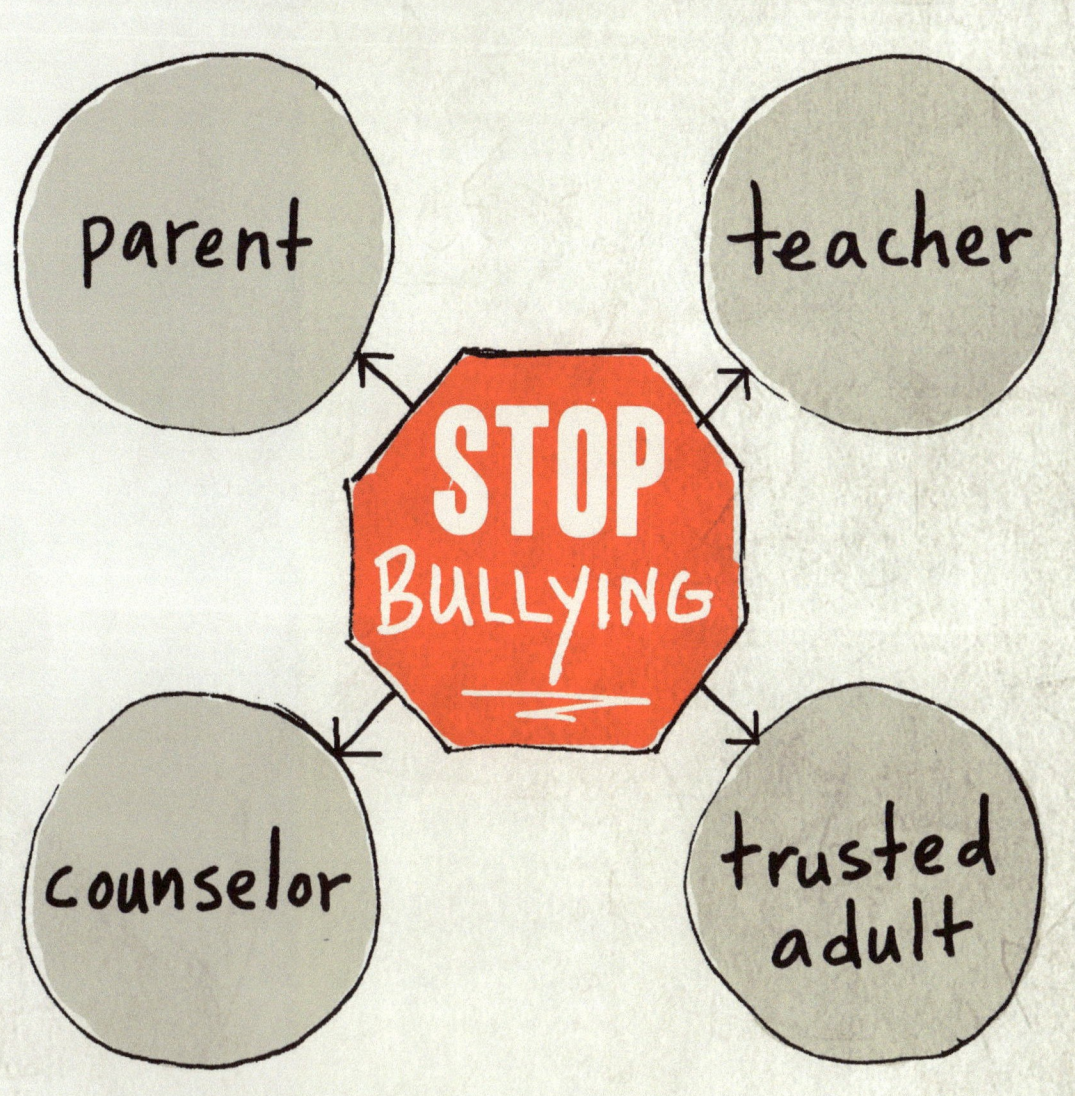

When you get caught
for bullying,
 you...

   **- will be in trouble
   at school**

   **- might have your
   toys taken away**

   **- might not be able
   to play sports**

   - might lose friends

and worst of all
- you will hurt someone else!!!

Are you listening?

When you bully someone, you...

- make them feel bad about themself

- make them not want to be your friend

- make them think you are mean

Why do people bully?

It can be because...

- sometimes they are sad

- they might feel alone

- they can be angry

- they think they can get away with it

- their friends do it too
    or maybe...

- they have been or
  are being bullied too

 Actually, I was bullied last year by an upper classman. Boy did it hurt!

 I bully in places I can get attention or I think I can make people laugh.

Bullying can
take place anywhere...

- **in your classroom**
- **on the playground**
- **in the hallways**

or even...

-**on the bus**

I bullied Connor in the cafeteria.
But nobody laughed like I thought
they would.

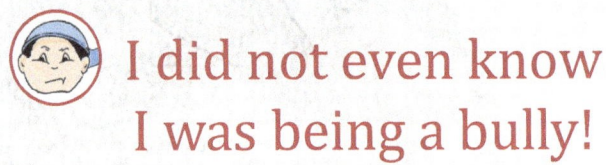 **I did not even know
I was being a bully!**

I realized after I found out that
bullying can be through

TOUCH   or   **TALK**

pushing	name calling
punching	spreading rumors
shoving	teasing
kicking	yelling
tripping	laughing at someone to hurt their feelings
slapping	

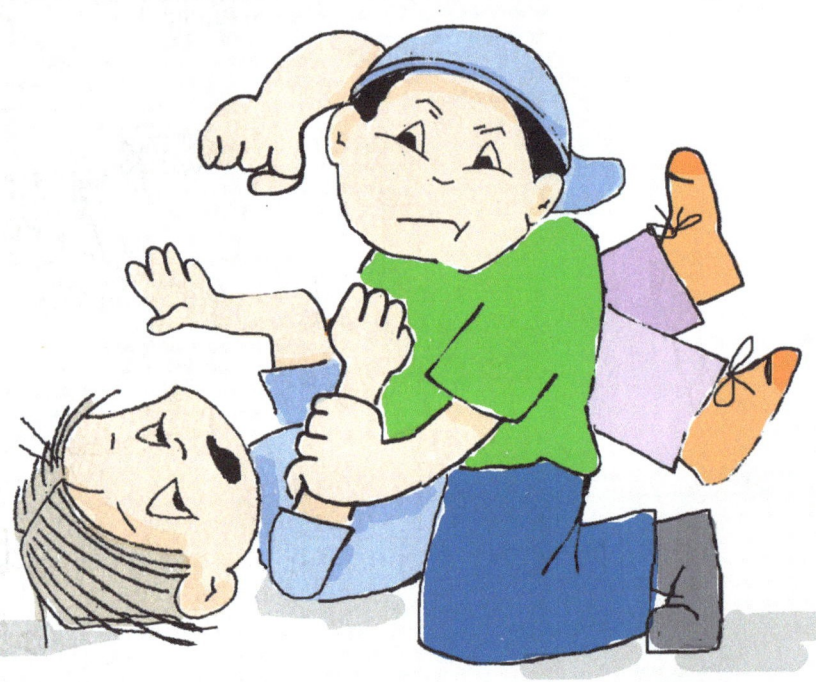

Bullies come in all colors, shapes and sizes.

Both boys and girls can be bullies.

What is bullying?

Bullying is when someone or a group of people purposely hurt another person through talk or touch. It is also when the person being bullied feels alone, scared and has trouble standing up for themself. The bully may also feel alone and may take his or her sadness out on others.

 **Hi!**

**My name is Gus!
I got in trouble for being a bully.**

Do you know what bullying means?

www.ingramcontent.com/pod-product-compliance
Lightning Source LLC
Chambersburg PA
CBHW042147290426
44110CB00003B/139